MW00889483

THIS PAGE
INTENTIONALLY
LEFT BLANK

PHRASAL VERBS
IN CONTEXT

RAONI ZANOVELLO

ENGLISH YOU KNOW

PHRASAL VERBS IN CONTEXT by RAONI D. ZANOVELLO

Published by EnglishYouKnow Books

San Francisco, California 94121

Cover by Raoni Zanovello

raoni@englishyouknow.com

Instagram @English.youknow

TikTok @English.youknow

Printed in the United States of America

Second Edition

ISBN 9798392226566

CONTENTS

This is hands-on material. It's a very straightforward book that invites you to be the main actor in your language-learning journey.

I have developed this book thoughtfully and thoroughly, thinking about useful applications for common high-frequency phrasal verbs in both spoken and written English.

One of the key attributes of this workbook is that it has a phonic approach. As you may know, English is not a phonetic language.

Phonetic languages are languages with a direct relationship between spelling and sound. This book includes audio resources.

Speaking is often one of the biggest obstacles English learners face. Based on my experience as an English teacher, it's very evident that most students adopt a passive learning style.

I encourage you to come to the active side of the learning process. Writing and reading aloud are highly encouraged throughout the exercises.

B. WHAT ARE PHRASAL VERBS?

A phrasal verb is a phrase that consists of a verb and one or more additional words, frequently a preposition but occasionally an adverb.

The meaning will vary even if the same word can be employed in numerous phrasal verbs, such as cut off, cut in, and cut out.

Therefore, it's critical to comprehend what verbs, prepositions, and adverbs are before discussing English phrasal verbs.

The book IS **MEANT FOR INTERMEDIATE STUDENTS**. It focuses on a range of vocabulary that is widely spoken in English and that learners should use.

The book may be of some help to some advanced students who struggle with conversational English. The book is not appropriate for beginners.

The phrasal verbs are set in FREQUENCY of usage in English. It's not necessary to go after every single one of them. use this as a workbook for memorizing and actively USING the NEWLY acquired vocabulary.

B. WHAT ARE PHRASAL VERBS?

'Should I really study phrasal verbs?' You may be thinking about whether it's relevant or not. The simple answer is yes. In English, particularly in spoken English, phrasal verbs are quite prevalent.

To assist you grasp what people are saying and to make yourself understood by others, you need to be familiar with frequent phrasal verbs.

Although phrasal verbs frequently have one-word verb equivalents (extinguish = put out, for example), those substitutes typically have a far more formal register than phrasal verbs. The usage of **phrasal verbs** and the proper level of formality can be seen in the examples below.

Hi! Happy you could **come along!**
Hi! Happy you could **attend!**

I'm sorry for **turning up** so late!
Sorry for **appearing** so late!

I **got on** the wrong train and then I got lost **looking for** your street.
I **boarded** the wrong train and then I got lost **seeking** your street.

Can I **take** my shoes **off**?
Can I **remove** my shoes?

Do you want something to drink before we **head off**? Water? Coffee?
Do you want something to drink before we **depart**? Water? Coffee?

I START VERY EARLY IN THE MORNING

My alarm **goes off(1)** at 6:00. I **wake up(2)**, **lean over(3)** and **turn off(4)** the alarm.

I **get up(5)** quickly and go to the bathroom.

I go to the kitchen to **put on(6)** the coffee.

I **go back(7)** to the bathroom to have a quick shower. I **put on(8)** my clothes.

I **come back(9)** to the kitchen to have an extra cup of coffee.

I wash my cup and **tidy up(10)** the kitchen.

I take my backpack and **set off(11)** to work. It is 7 am.

I **lock up(12)** the house before I leave.

I **get in(13)** the car and **drive off(14)** to work.

I **get on(15)** well with my colleagues, they're all very friendly.

1. **Goes off –** makes a loud noise
2. **wake up –** no longer sleeping
3. **lean over –** reach the alarm clock
4. **turn off –** make the alarm stop
5. **get up** – stand on your feet
6. **put on –** serve the coffee
7. **go back –** return to the bathroom
8. **put on –** dress
9. **come back –** return to the kitchen
10. **tidy up –** make the kitchen clean and organized
11. **set off –** leave
12. **lock up –** lock the door
13. **get in –** enter the car
14. **drive off –** start driving
15. **get on –** have a good relationship

Phrasal verbs can be **separable** or **inseparable**, **transitive** or **intransitive**.

Transitive or Intransitive

Transitive

The thing or person being acted on is the direct object of transitive phrasal verbs. Take the phrasal verb "put on," for instance:

*Actors need to **put on** some makeup before acting.*

The makeup is the direct object in that sentence. You cannot say "Actors need to put on some makeup before acting. A direct object is required for transitive verbs. What exactly do actors need to put on?

A few more examples of transitive phrasal verbs:

*We need to **take off** our shoes when we get inside.*
*We need to **work out** a solution for our problems.*

Intransitive

In this case, direct objects are absent from intransitive phrasal verbs.
They can be used directly in a sentence:

*In the winter is easy to go to bed but hard to **get up**.*
*My friends want to **hang out** at this new cafe that just opened.*

C. TYPES OF PHRASAL VERBS

Separable or Inseparable

Separable

Phrasal verbs that can be divided apart by adding a word or phrase in the middle are called separable phrasal verbs:

> You weren't at the meeting yesterday, but don't worry. I'll **fill** you **in**.
> The heater was on so I really had to **take** my jacket **off**. It was just too hot.

Separable phrasal verbs are transitive by definition; the direct object is what gets placed in the middle of the phrase. Usually, the word order is a little more lenient when the direct object is a noun. You can either add it after the phrasal verb or put it inside of it:

> I'm going to **turn off** my phone because I need to concentrate now.
> I'm going to **turn** my phone **off** because I need to concentrate now.

Exception: if the direct object is a pronoun (he, she, it, you, them) it would have to be added to the phrasal verb:

> **Correct**: We brought a pizza to **cheer** him **up**.
> **Incorrect**: We brought a pizza to cheer up him.

8

Separable or Inseparable

Inseparable

You can't separate phrasal verbs that are inseparable! Even if it is a pronoun, the direct object must follow after the phrasal verb.

> **Correct**: You need to **show up** on time at work.
>
> **Incorrect**: You need to show on time at work up.

Phrasal verbs that cannot be separated can be either transitive or intransitive:

> She **came across** some old photographs in a drawer. (transitive)
>
> All plants like to **grow up** in the direction of the sunlight. (intransitive)

The problem is that it's difficult to determine whether a phrasal verb is separable or inseparable; instead, you must pay attention to how it is utilized if you come across a new phrasal word.

English phrasal verbs are often used, thus hearing them in a conversation is not unusual.

Do you frequently hear a verb and another noun together? Perhaps it is a phrasal verb.

Try checking up a phrase if you're unsure of whether it's a phrasal verb or simply a verb that occurred to be pronounced with a preposition.

Look up the phrase in a dictionary to be sure because phrasal verbs are typically included there.

While some phrasal verb meanings, such as "fall down," are evident, others resemble idioms because they cannot be translated literally.

You might try categorizing the phrasal verbs to make them simpler to learn, You may, for instance, group phrasal verbs.

Phrasal verbs can be used whenever they make sense, just like verbs.

The first thing to keep in mind is whether a phrasal verb is separable or not. When using an inseparable verb, such as "fall down," the verb and preposition must be stated jointly.

However, you can also separate the verb and the preposition for separable verbs by inserting another word in between them. Therefore, you can either say "turn off the TV" or "turn the TV off." Both are true.

Phrasal verbs are still verbs, which is another thing to remember. Accordingly, the verb in the phrase can vary based on the sentence's tense and subject.

So "turn off" can transform like this:

*I **turned on** the radio this morning.*
*He **turns** the radio **on** every time I get in the room!*

F. PROBLEMS ENGLISH LEARNERS FACE

For non-native English speakers, phrasal verbs (such as "look up" and "find out") offer various difficulties. In this post, we'll go through those difficulties, provide some advice on how to deal with them, and provide exercises and resources you can use to advance your command of these verbs.

PROBLEM 1
THEY'RE DIFFICULT TO SPOT

Because they consist of a primary verb and one or more particles, phrasal verbs can be challenging to identify.

Break down is equal to break (*main verb*) + down (*particle*)
Put up with is the same as putting (*main verb*) up (*particle 1*) with (*particle 2*)

The words "in," "out," "on," and "away," among others, are examples of particles. However, they function as a part of the verb rather than as prepositions or adverbs.

Let's examine a case:

> ## They run up the street.
> verb **run** + "up the street" as a preposition
>
> ## She ran up a big bill at a hotel.
> phrasal verb

The main verb in the first sentence is "run," while the phrase "up the street" refers to the direction they ran in.

The verb "run up" is a phrasal verb that is employed in the second sentence. *"We stayed too long in this hotel and ran up the bill."*
"Run up" in this context indicates a great increase.

But if you **aren't familiar** with that phrase, it can be **challenging to tell that a phrasal verb is being used** because these two sentences appear to be extremely similar.

PROBLEM 2
THEY CAN HAVE SEVERAL MEANINGS

It's common to find a lengthy list of definitions for phrasal verbs in dictionaries. According to one study, phrasal verbs that are frequently used have an average of 5.6 meanings (Gardner and Davies, 2007). Therefore, if you wish to study a list of 20 phrasal verbs, you actually need to memorize almost 100 definitions!

THEY LOOK ALMOST LIKE EACH OTHER

The structures of many phrasal verbs are comparable.

As an illustration, here are a few using the primary verb come:

Come on, come on with, come back,
come down with, come in, come up, come out, etc.

Numerous phrasal verbs employ the same particles as well:
come on, hit on, toss on, put on, take on, etc.

Because of this, it can be very simple to misuse phrasal verbs and say something other than what you mean.

PROBLEM 4
UNUSUAL GRAMMAR

Phrasal verbs virtually resemble one-word verbs when all the parts are present:

On the side of the road, the car broke down.
In my book, I looked up the word.

But they don't always seem this way, as you've probably seen. Others are non-separable and must remain intact, whereas other phrasal verbs can be divided and let other words appear in the spaces.

The rules for separation depend on whether the verb has a direct object and whether the direct object is a pronoun. We'll save those details for another post, but just know that those rules can produce sentences like the following:

The car broke down on the side of the road.
I broke down the problem step-by-step.
I broke the problem down step-by-step.
I broke it down step-by-step.
But the sentences below are generally viewed as incorrect.
I broke down it step-by-step.
The car broke on the side of the road down.

PROBLEM 5
PHRASAL VERBS ARE OFTEN IDIOMATIC

"Idiomatic" refers to a word combination that conveys a meaning other than what you may anticipate from its constituent parts. Even if you've never heard of them before, some phrasal verbs are fairly literal and simple to understand:

*Can you **fill up** my coffee?*
Please refill my coffee.

Even if you've never heard the phrase "fill up," you can probably guess that it means something along the line "fill entirely."

On the other hand, idiomatic phrasal verbs can be more challenging to comprehend if you've never encountered them.

I believe I will simply give up.

In the example above, "give up" refers to "stop trying," yet the combination of "give" and "up" does not instantly convey this meaning.

So it's quite understandable if these difficulties have you trying to avoid utilizing phrasal verbs when you talk. Although they are among the most difficult vocabulary items in English to learn and master, if you put some time into practicing these crucial verbs, it should be simpler for you to speak the language fluently.

Last few tips before we get down to business

TIP 1

As you learn new phrasal verbs, consider how YOU will use them. Put those phrasal verbs in writing and keep reviewing any sentences or phrases you might use in the future. Here in this book, you will find plenty of space for writing practice. Technology can be convenient, but our brains need time to digest new information. Writing is still the most effective learning method to date. No miracle app will help you retain information nearly as effectively as writing. Remember, your ability to employ the new terms you learned can significantly improve with just a few minutes a day of reviewing.

TIP 2

Look up definitions and illustrations on the internet. Finally, consult a thorough reference to look up and observe the usage of phrasal verbs. Longman's dictionary is a simple and effective dictionary that can help you in your learning process. There are others too, like Oxford's Learner and Cambridge Dictionary.

PHRASAL VERBS
VERBS
IN CONTEXT

Read the text below. Pay attention the phrasal verbs in bold.

A HECTIC MORNING

On my way to work, my car **breaks down**.
I call my manager to tell him we may have to **call off** the meeting as I'm the person who prepared the main presentation.

My boss **brings up** that the company's executives are going to be there, then tells me to **calm down** and try my best to get there as soon as possible:

"I'll make some time for you to **catch up**." He says.

I apologize to my boss and **hang up** the phone. I'm standing next to my car on a busy road, waiting for the insurance company.

A police officer **comes across**. He says 'hi' with a smile and **comes across** as a very friendly officer.

He advises me to push my car onto the shoulder as he offers me a hand.

I don't feel like waiting for the insurance company. Because of that, I ask the police officer if he thinks this part of town is safe.
He, in turn, tells me that burglars **break in** regularly in that area.

I tell him that I really have to **carry on** with my day. That officer really **came across** as a nice person. He seems to **be into** helping the community.

He tells me that he'll wait for the insurance company for me. I thank him. I **get in** a taxi and **check out** from the scene. While I'm in the taxi, Carol messages me, **asking** me **out**!

I get super excited for a minute and forget about the situation, then I tell her I'd love to **go out**, and quickly summarize my morning.
She tells me that this whole story doesn't add **up**; I agree with her in return, but it really feels like I'm lying.

We schedule something for Friday night and **hang up** the phone.

TURN THE PAGE

A HECTIC MORNING

I get to the office on time but I still feel that I need to **brush up** *on* my presentation. But there's no point in that. **Brushing up** *on* things takes time.

I just couldn't do that. I was running out of time.

Now I'm at my boss' office telling him I think I can't do it.
My boss tells me that I'm going to do great.

I tell myself that I know that there's no way to **back down** at this point. **Chickening out** is not an option. I can do this. I have everything **figured out**.

Jenny **breaks in** with a message from the main office "They **came about** a problem with the investors and are now **calling off** our meeting.
The investors said that the numbers *don't* **add up**."

How did all that **come about**? It's been such a chaotic morning.
I feel **beat up** already!

I just couldn't do that. I was running out of time.

Now I'm at my boss' office telling him I think I can't do it.
My boss tells me that I'm going to do great.

I tell myself that I know that there's no way to **back down** at this point. **Chickening out** is not an option. I can do this. I have everything **figured out.**

Jenny **breaks in** with a message from the main office "They **came about** a problem with the investors and are now **calling off** our meeting. The investors said that the numbers *don't* **add up**."

How did all that **come about**? It's been such a chaotic morning.
I feel **beat up** already!

BEFORE WE PROCEED

1. ALL OF THE EXERCISES SHOULD BE REVIEWED AND DONE IN AN SPACED TIME.
2. **DO NOT DO ALL THE EXERCISES ALL AT ONCE.**
3. **REMEMBER: UNDERSTANDING IS NOT INTERNALIZING.**
4. WE NEED SOME REPETITION.

I SUGGEST YOU USE YOUR CREATIVITY TO IMAGINE AND THINK ABOUT NEWLY ACQUIRED VOCABULARY IN ORDER TO HAVE BETTER VOCABULARY RETENTION.

Oral Text 1 (part 1/3)
A Hectic Morning

On my way to work, my car **breaks down(1)**.
I call my manager to tell him we may have to **call off(2)** the meeting as I'm the person who prepared the main presentation.

My boss **brings up(3)** that the company's executives are going to be there, then tells me to **calm down(4)** and try my best to get there as soon as possible:

"I'll make some time for you to **catch up(5)**". He says.

I apologize to my boss and **hang up(6)** the phone. I'm standing next to my car on a busy road, waiting for the insurance company.

A police officer **comes across(7)**. He says 'hi' with a smile and **comes across(8)** as a very friendly officer.

He advises me to push my car onto the shoulder as he offers me a hand.

I don't feel like waiting for the insurance company. Because of that, I ask the police officer if he thinks this part of town is safe.
He in return tells me that burglars **break in(9)** regularly in that area.

I tell him that I really have to **carry on(10)** with my day. That officer really **came across(11)** as a nice person. He seems to **be into(12)** helping the community.

---

breaks down(1) - stop working
call off(2) - cancel
brings up(3) - mention something (usually something important)
calm down(4) - to relax
catch up(5) - to understand or to reach someone or something
hang up(6) - to finish a call
comes across(7) - to appear unexpectedly
comes across(8) - to be seen as friendly
break in(9) - to break the window and rob something
carry on(10) - to continue
came across(11) - be perceived as a nice person
be into(12) - to enjoy/to like something

If a machine or vehicle **breaks down**, it stops working. If a relationship or a system **breaks down**, it fails, or it's failing due to a problem or discrepancy.

To **break down** *something*, or to **break** *something* **down** can also mean to separate things into smaller parts so that they can be more easily understood or dealt with. If *someone* **breaks down**, they may experience emotional distress and, if *something* is **broken down**, it may fall onto the ground.

EXAMPLE:

My car **broke down** yesterday, I'm taking a bus now.

My relationship **broke down** because we didn't communicate.

The report **broke down** the election result.

If you **call off** a meeting you cancel a meeting. Call off can also mean to reduce. If you call off someone or something, you ask that person to leave the specific place they're at.

*His attention was **called off** when his ex-wife arrived.*

EXAMPLE:

Greenpeace refused to **call off** the event.

Don't let anything **call off** your attention from your studies.

Please **call off** the dog; it's barking at the children.

Don't let anything call off your attention from your studies.

Write three sentences.

_____

_____

_____

_____

To talk about a topic or mention a topic. To vomit something. To look after a child until it is an adult.

EXAMPLE:

He was brought up by his grandparents.

She ran to the hospital because she brought up blood.

When you see Mary, don't bring up her divorce. She is very sad about it.

What are you waiting for?
Bring up three sentences down below.

_____

_____

_____

_____

CALM DOWN

To relax or to get to a point where things are calmer than before.

EXAMPLE:

Calm down for a minute and listen to me.

Calm down and think carefully.

We just need to wait for the situation to **calm down**.

Calm down and think carefully.
Calmly write three sentences using 'calm down.'

_____

_____

_____

_____

Catch up has different meanings:

If you are **caught up** in *something*, you are involved in it, usually unwillingly.

If you **catch up** on friends whom you have not seen for some time. You talk to them and **find out** what has happened in their lives since you last talked together;

If you **catch up** *with someone* who is in front of you, you reach them by walking faster than they are walking; to **catch up** with *someone* means to reach the same standard, stage, or level that they have reached;

If you **catch up** *on* an activity that you have not had much time to do recently, you spend time doing it;

I waited so she could **catch** *me* **up**.

We **caught up** with the others after 2 kilometers.

Let's talk soon! We have a lot of things to **catch up** on.

He was **catching up** on reading during the lockdown.

Steve wasn't involved in the fight, but he got **caught up** in it.

He's **catching up** on Math.

Sergio is an expert and I am not. It's hard to **catch up** with his thinking.

I enrolled later, so I had to work hard to **catch up** with my classmates.

Are you all caught up? Write three sentences to break free.

If you feel like you're not catching up, keep running.

_____

_____

_____

_____

6 HANG UP

Someone is calling.
I need to pick up the phone.

It was a seller,
I told him that I had
to hang up the phone.

The shirts are hanging.

The girl is hanging up
the clothes.

If you **come across** *somebody/something,* you find or discover someone or something by chance. An idea that comes across is **easy for people to understand**. Come across can also mean having specific traits or qualities.

I **came across** *some old photographs* in his drawer.
(found by chance)

He **came across** *an old friend. (met by chance)*
Your *speech* **came across** very well. *(easy to understand)*
She **comes across** as a very bright woman. *(she is perceived)*
Your *point* **came across** at the meeting. *(easy to understand your points)*

Was this phrasal verb easy to come across?

Or was it hard to come across?

_____

_____

_____

_____

If someone breaks in they get inside a house or a building by force.

Break in can also be used figuratively, if someone interrupts you they are breaking in.

EXAMPLE:

Dad would occasionally **break in** with a funny comment.

Thieves **broke in** and ripped off five computers.

She waited for a **break in** the conversation.

Avoid getting caught by writing three sentences!

_____

_____

_____

_____

CARRY ON

To continue doing something.

EXAMPLE:

Let's **carry on** this discussion at some other time.

Carry on until you get to the junction, then turn left.

He wanted an heir to **carry on** the family name.

Carry on with your English studies.
Three sentences are needed below.

_____

_____

_____

_____

11 COME ACROSS

see 7/8 pg. X

BE INTO

To be into means to like or to be interested in something or someone.

EXAMPLE:

Joseph **is** really **into** Jenny, but he won't tell her.

He **was into** soccer, but he is out of form and doesn't play anymore.

He **is** really **into** exercising. He goes to the gym every day.

I'm really into phrasal verbs.
What about you?

_____

_____

_____

_____

Oral Text 1 (part 2/3)
A Hectic Morning

He tells me that he'll wait for the insurance company for me. I thank him. I **get in(13)** a taxi and **check out(14)** from the scene. While I'm in the taxi Carol messages me **asking** me **out(15)**!

I get super excited for a minute and forget about the situation, then I tell her I'd love to **go out(16)**, and quickly summarize my morning.
She tells me that this whole story doesn't **add up(17)**; I agree with her in return, but it really feels like I'm lying.

We schedule something for Friday night and **hang up(18)** the phone.

I get to the office on time but I still feel that I need to **brush up(19)** *on* my presentation. But there's no point in that. **Brushing up(20)** *on* things takes time.

I just couldn't do that. I was running out of time.

Now I'm at my boss' office telling him I think I can't do it.
My boss tells me that I'm going to do great.

I tell myself that I know that there's no way to **back down(21)** at this point. **Chickening out(22)** is not an option. I can do this. I have everything **figured out(23)**.

Jenny **breaks in(24)** with a message from the main office "They **came about(25)** a problem with the investors and are now **calling off(26)** our meeting. The investors said that the numbers *don't* **add up(27)**."

How did all that **come about(28)**? It's been such a chaotic morning.
I feel **beat up(29)** already!

Get in(13) - enter the taxi
Check out(14) - leave/remove yourself from the scene
Ask out(15) - carol asks if he wants to go out with her
Go out(16) - to go somewhere with friends or on a date
Add up(17) - this story seems like a lie
Hang up(18) - we scheduled something for Friday night and finished the call
Brush up *(on)***(19) -** I need to revise my presentation
Brush up *(on)***(20) -** refining something takes time

TO ENTER

got in; got in or gotten in; getting in; gets in

intransitive verb

ENTER, ARRIVE, to become friendly, to become involved

it will be late when you get in, so you may have trouble finding a taxi.

Tickets for kids 5 to 12 years old are $10, and children under 5 get in for free.

When heading out for a run or a walk, a bra and bike shorts pairing is sure not to get in your way.

To check out at a hotel is to leave the hotel. The same idea for when you're buying groceries at a supermarket when you're at the cashier, you're checking out. Confusingly, **checking out** can also mean looking at something or to get more information about something. **Check out** is casual. Avoid using this term in formal settings.

The police had to **check out** the call.

Check out the prices at our new store!

We're supposed to **check out** of the hotel by 11 o'clock.

Write three sentences with check out before you check out.

_____

_____

_____

_____

15 ASK OUT

Ask *someone* **out** is an invitation for a date.

EXAMPLE:

I guess he **asked** *her* **out**.

Did you ask *her* **out**? What did she say?

He **asked** *me* **OUT** and I said yes.

Have you ever asked people out?
How did it go?

_____

_____

_____

_____

To **go out** can have several meanings. You can be referring to a light that you need to turn off. If you go out with someone, you're dating that person romantically.

A few minutes later the lights went out. (the light was turned off)

The tide was going out. (ebb; recede to low tide.)

ADD UP

His story doesn't add up!

An Event or a fact that *doesn't* **add up** creates confusion or is inconsistent. If a fact or event **adds up**, it is consistent and reasonable.

EXAMPLE:

The various facts in this case just **don't add up**.

His promises don't **add up**.

Her story doesn't **add up**. I think he is lying.

I'm not sure, but it seems that what he said **adds up**.

Great to add up new words! Add up three sentences down below!

_____

_____

_____

_____

REFRESHER:

Hang up means to end a phone call or
to hang something.

**I have to hang up my clothes after I hang
up the phone.**

BRUSH UP (ON)

If you brush up on something you practice and improve your skills or knowledge.

Example:

I need to brush up on my computer skills.

I need to brush up on my English.

Public libraries have computers people can use to brush up on their skills.

Brush up your writing by writing three sentences.

_____

_____

_____

_____

Oral Text 1 (part 3/3)
A Hectic Morning

I just couldn't do that. I was running out of time.

Now I'm at my boss' office telling him I think I can't do it.
My boss tells me that I'm going to do great.

I tell myself that I know that there's no way to **back down(21)** at this point. **Chickening out(22)** is not an option. I can do this. I have everything **figured out(23)**.

Jenny **breaks in(24)** with a message from the main office "They **came about(25)** a problem with the investors and are now **calling off(26)** our meeting. The investors said that the numbers *don't* **add up(27)**."

How did all that **come about(28)**? It's been such a chaotic morning.
I feel **beat up(29)** already!

Back down(21) - to surrender or to concede
Chickening out(22) - being afraid is not an option
Figured out(23) - I have everything ready
Breaks in (24) - Jane interrupts
Came about (25) -they found a problem
Calling off(26) - cancel the meeting
Add up(27) - the numbers don't make sense
Come about(28) - how did all that happen
Beat up(29) - I feel extremely tired already

21 BACK DOWN

If you **back down** that means that you surrender or conceal.

EXAMPLE:

It's too late to **back down** now.

They refused to **back down**.

She refused to **back down** on a point of principle.

Do not back down, you can do this!

Write three sentences.

_____

_____

_____

_____

If you are too frightened and decide not to do something because of that.

EXAMPLE:

The boy **chickened out** of climbing up the tree.

He **chickened out** at the last moment.

If I don't fight him, everyone will say that I **chickened out**.

You writing those three sentences, right?

You're not chickening out, are you?

_____

_____

_____

_____

If you figure out a solution to a problem or the reason for something, you succeed in solving it or understanding it.

E.g.:

It took me one week to figure out how to solve this math problem. Among us is a game in which 8 people have to complete tasks and figure out who are the two impostors, and 2 people have to kill everyone and pretend to be innocent.

People are trying to figure out how to adjust to the pandemic.

_____

_____

_____

_____

BREAK IN

Can you use the noun form of the phrasal

verb BREAK IN?

Break-in (noun)

Break in (phrasal verb)

_____

_____

_____

_____

COME ABOUT

Come about Is when something happens, especially if it's not planned.

EXAMPLE:

The opportunity to get into arts **came about** by accident.

It's hard to understand how the accident **came about**.

The flood **came about** as a result of the heavy spring rains.

How did it **come about** that she married an awful man like that?

How did this situation **come about**?

Someone has been murdered in mysterious circumstances: how has it **come about**?

~~Can you remember three events in your life that came about?~~

_____

_____

_____

CALL OFF

CAN YOU STILL REMEMBER

CALL OFF FROM REFERENCE 3?

Do you think you can come up with a sentence

using its noun form?

Call off (phrasal verb)

Call-off (noun)

_____

_____

_____

_____

ADD UP

Refresher

Do you still remember the phrasal verb add up?

How about writing down a few synonyms

and put it into context using your own

original sentences?

_____

_____

_____

_____

COME ABOUT

GO TO REFERENCE 25

BEAT UP

If someone **beats** *a person* **up**, they hit or kick the person many times, and If you **beat** *yourself* **up** about something, you feel concerned about that thing a lot or blame yourself for that specific thing.

EXAMPLE:

Her boyfriend got drunk and **beat** <u>her</u> **up**.

John got **beaten up** outside the nightclub this Friday night.

Some violent men **beat up** their sons until the boys are strong enough to hit back.

Are phrasal verbs beating you up? I hope not.

_____

_____

_____

_____

PHRASAL VERBS WITH **TAKE**

Sometimes it's hard to **take in**(1) what my English teacher says. I've been learning English for 4 months now. When I become fluent in English, I'll **take up**(2) French lessons.

In my first lesson, I noticed my printed English book was defective, so I had to **take** *it* **back**(3) to the bookstore. The bookstore was a bit far from my home, but it wasn't entirely bad, because I was **taking** *my girlfriend* **out**(4) for dinner in a restaurant close by.

And by the way... I'm taking her out because she **took away**(5) my video game as she was saying I wasn't giving her enough attention. "You **took to**(6) playing all night after work, and that's terrible!"

I agree with her, but sometimes I just feel like she's trying to **take over**(7). After meeting her parents I can tell she **takes after**(8) her mother. She is so controlling!

1-absorb, notice, and understand
2-start to do something new, like a hobby, a school subject...
3-return something
4-invite and go out with someone
5-remove something and take it with you when you leave
6-create or fall into a habit
7-to take control of a situation, someone, or something
8-to look like or behave like someone in your family

FILL IN THE GAPS WITH THE OPTIONS BELOW.

I've been reading classic literature. Sometimes I feel like it's just too much. Some parts are really hard to take _ _ _ _.

I've been wasting so much time playing games online. I need to take _ _ _ _ a new pastime.

This phone is completely defective. I'll have to take it _ _ _ _ to the store.

I can't believe Marcos is taking me _ _ _ _ tonight. I'm so excited!

When I was younger my mom would always take _ _ _ _ toys if I didn't behave well.

Recently I've taken _ _ _ _ smoke.

My wife is very controlling, she's always trying to take _ _ _ _.

Everybody says I take _ _ _ _ my mom.

AFTER. OVER. TO. AWAY. OUT. BACK. UP. IN.

PHRASAL VERBS WITH COME

My father is **coming down**(1) this weekend. They're **coming from**(2) another state. I finished work earlier to be able to **come back**(3) home faster and meet them upon their arrival.

When I met with my dad the first thing he said was "**Come on**!(4) Someone needs to put a leash on your neighbor's dog! He almost **came at**(5) me."

That's terrible dad... but how are you? Please, **come in**(6)!
Listen, I was planning on picking up my wife at work. Want to **come along**(7)? And by the way... I **came across**(8) some old photographs in my basement from your wedding. Do you want them back?

1- visiting from a different place
2- a place of origin
3- to return
4- an expression to say something is not right
5- tried to attack
6- to enter; to arrive
7- to go somewhere with somebody
8- to find something by accident or without expecting it

FILL IN THE GAPS WITH THE OPTIONS BELOW.

Let's Practice!

Come _ _ _ _ ! You're gonna be late!

My family comes _ _ _ _ _ my career.

My parents are coming _ _ _ _ the holidays.

I finished work earlier and came _ _ _ _ home.

The neighbor's dog wanted to come _ _ _ _ me.

We're getting some burgers. Want to come _ _ _ _?

I came _ _ _ _ _ some old photographs in the basement.

I'm glad you came! Please, come _ _ _ _!

ON. BEFORE. DOWN. BACK. AT. ALONG. ACROSS. IN.

MORE PHRASAL VERBS

WATCH THIS VIDEO

Flip up: To raise or lift something with a quick movement.

Example: She flipped up the hood of her jacket to protect from the rain.

Burst into: To suddenly enter a place, often with a lot of energy or noise.

Example: The children burst into the room, excited to see their presents.

Take off: To remove or remove from a surface.

Example: She took off her shoes and relaxed on the couch.

Peel off: To remove a layer of something by pulling it away.

Example: He peeled off the label from the bottle.

Twist off: To remove by twisting.

Example: She twisted off the cap of the bottle.

Crack open: To open something by applying force, especially with a sharp sound.

Example: He cracked open the walnut with a nutcracker.

MORE PHRASAL VERBS

Can you answer off the top of your head?

Samantha was on a hike in the mountains and as she reached the summit, she heard a loud noise. She quickly flipped __ the hood of her jacket to protect from the rain and burst ____ a clearing, where she saw a bird stuck in a trap.

She took ___ her backpack and started to look for something to help the bird. She found a rock and used it to peel ___ the trap from the bird's foot.

The bird was so grateful and as a token of appreciation, it gave Samantha a bottle of rare nectar. She twisted ___ the cap of the bottle and took a sip.

It was the sweetest nectar she had ever tasted. She decided to crack ____ the bottle and share it with her friends. They all sat together and enjoyed the drink, while the bird flew ____ into the sky.

KEY

Samantha was on a hike in the mountains and as she reached the summit, she heard a loud noise. She quickly (flip up) the hood of her jacket to protect from the rain and (burst into) a clearing, where she saw a bird stuck in a trap. She (took off) her backpack and started to look for something to help the bird. She found a rock and used it to (peel off) the trap from the bird's foot. The bird was so grateful and as a token of appreciation, it gave Samantha a bottle of rare nectar. She (twisted off) the cap of the bottle and took a sip. It was the sweetest nectar she had ever tasted. She decided to (crack open) the bottle and share it with her friends. They all sat together and enjoyed the drink, while the bird flew away into the sky.

MORE PHRASAL VERBS

Samantha was on a hike in the mountains and as she reached the summit, she heard a loud noise. She quickly flipped __ the hood of her jacket to protect from the rain and burst ____ a clearing, where she saw a bird stuck in a trap.

She took ___ her backpack and started to look for something to help the bird. She found a rock and used it to peel ___ the trap from the bird's foot.

The bird was so grateful and as a token of appreciation, it gave Samantha a bottle of rare nectar. She twisted ___ the cap of the bottle and took a sip.

It was the sweetest nectar she had ever tasted. She decided to crack ____ the bottle and share it with her friends. They all sat together and enjoyed the drink, while the bird flew ____ into the sky.

KEY

Samantha was on a hike in the mountains and as she reached the summit, she heard a loud noise. She quickly (flip up) the hood of her jacket to protect from the rain and (burst into) a clearing, where she saw a bird stuck in a trap. She (took off) her backpack and started to look for something to help the bird. She found a rock and used it to (peel off) the trap from the bird's foot. The bird was so grateful and as a token of appreciation, it gave Samantha a bottle of rare nectar. She (twisted off) the cap of the bottle and took a sip. It was the sweetest nectar she had ever tasted. She decided to (crack open) the bottle and share it with her friends. They all sat together and enjoyed the drink, while the bird flew away into the sky.

1 - A piece of cake:

something that is very easy to do.

ORIGIN

The exact origin of the idiom "a piece of cake" is uncertain, but there are a few theories.

One theory suggests that the phrase may have originated from the practice of giving cake as a reward for completing a task in the early 1900s.

Another theory suggests that it may have come from the idea of dividing a cake into equal pieces, which is an easy task.

Another theory suggests that it may have originated from the Royal Air Force during World War II. The story goes that pilots would describe an easy mission as "a piece of cake," and this phrase eventually caught on in popular usage.

2 - Break a leg:

good luck in your performance

How to use it

Regardless of its origin, "break a leg" is now commonly used in the theater industry as a way of wishing someone good luck before a performance.

It is considered bad luck to say "good luck" directly, so "break a leg" has become a more acceptable alternative. The phrase is also sometimes used in other situations to wish someone success or to encourage them to do their best.

3 - to cost an arm and a leg

to be very expensive

That designer dress costs an arm and a leg.

Possible Origin

"Cost an arm and a leg" is an expression that means something is very expensive. T

here are a few theories about where this expression comes from, but nobody knows for sure.

One idea is that it originated from the practice of charging different prices for portraits based on how much of the subject's body was included in the painting.

If someone wanted a full-length portrait, it would cost them a lot of money, or "an arm and a leg."

Another theory is that it came from soldiers in World War II receiving compensation payments for losing limbs.

Either way, the expression has become a common way to describe something that is very expensive.

4 - to cut corners

To do something in a hasty or incomplete manner.

Don't cut corners when it comes to safety regulations.

Origin

"Cut corners" originated from horse racing, where jockeys would take shortcuts by riding straight through the corners of a rectangular track.

This term now refers to taking shortcuts or avoiding proper procedures to save time or money, often at the expense of quality or safety.

5 - to the cat out of the bag

To reveal a secret or information that was hidden

She let the cat out of the bag about the surprise party.

Origin

The origin of the phrase is uncertain, but it may have come from scams in medieval markets, where sellers would pretend to sell a valuable animal, such as a pig, but would actually sell a cheaper animal, such as a cat.

BONUS IDIOMS

6 - On the ball

Being attentive and ready to take action.

You need to be on the ball to succeed in this job.

Origin

"On the ball" means being alert and efficient, and its origin is in sports, especially ball games like soccer, baseball, and basketball.

In those games, it's important to be fully focused and quick to react to any changes or opportunities.

The phrase has now become a common idiom used to describe someone who is quick, alert, and efficient in any situation.

7 - Piece of my mind

Speaking one's mind honestly and directly.

I'm going to give him a piece of my mind about his behavior.

Origin

The phrase "piece of mind" means giving someone a scolding or speaking your mind about something that has been bothering you.

It originated in the 16th century and referred to giving someone a portion of your thoughts, often in the form of criticism.

Today, it's a common expression used to describe expressing your dissatisfaction or disapproval of a situation.

It's a straightforward and often blunt way of communicating, but it can also be a way to clear the air and move forward.

66

8 - The whole nine yards

Everything or all the way.

He went the whole nine yards to plan the perfect party.

Origin

The phrase "whole nine yards" means giving something your all or going all out.

Its origin is uncertain, but it's commonly believed to come from either the length of a World War II fighter plane's ammunition belt or the construction industry's standard bolt of fabric, both of which were nine yards long.

The phrase is now a popular idiom used to express the idea of doing everything you can to achieve a goal or complete a task.

9 - Time flies

Time passes quickly.

It feels like yesterday when we started our freshman year, but now it's already graduation day. Time flies.

"Time flies" means that time seems to pass quickly or feel like it's moving faster than expected.

It's based on the idea that time passes quickly when you're enjoying yourself or engaged in fulfilling activities. It's a reminder to make the most of the time you have because it can feel like it's passing by quickly.

10 - Your guess is as good as mine

I have no idea.

How long is this meeting?

Your guess is as good as mine.

"Your guess is as good as mine" is a phrase used to convey that the speaker has no more information or knowledge about a particular situation or topic than the listener does.

It suggests that neither person knows the answer or solution, and they are both equally uncertain.

It's often used as a way to express that the speaker doesn't have any more information to share or that they can't offer any further insights.

It can also be used to indicate that the speaker is not willing to speculate or make guesses about the situation.

BONUS IDIOMS EXERCISE

Fill in the blank:

"Don't worry about the math test, it's going to be

_____."

Use this idiom to wish someone good luck:

"_____ on your job interview

tomorrow!"

Write a sentence that advises against taking shortcuts:

"If you _____, you may end up with a

shoddy end product."

Complete this sentence to express that something is very expensive:

"I really want to go on that vacation, but it's going to

_____."

Use this idiom to describe a situation where a secret is revealed:

"Why did you have to _____ about the

surprise party? Now everyone knows!"

BONUS IDIOMS EXERCISE

Write a sentence that describes someone who is very organized and efficient:

"My boss is always _ _ _ _ _ _ _ _ _ _ _ _ _ _ _ _, never missing a deadline or making a mistake."

Use this idiom to describe a feeling of relief or calmness:

"After submitting my project, I finally had a

_ _ _ _ _ _ _ _ _ _ _ _ _ _ about its quality."

Write a sentence that uses the idiom "the whole nine yards" to describe someone going all-out:

"For her wedding, my sister went _ _ _ _ _ _ _ _ _ _ _ _ _ _ _ _, with a fancy dress, a live band, and a gourmet caterer."

Use this idiom to express surprise at how quickly time has passed:

"I can't believe how fast _ _ _ _ _ _ _ _ _ _ _ _ _ _ _ _! It feels like just yesterday it was New Year's Day."

Complete this sentence to indicate uncertainty about a situation:

"Do you know what's going to happen next? Sorry,

_ _ _ _ _ _ _ _ _ _ _ _ _ _ _."

A JOURNEY THROUGH TIME

UNCOVERING THE ORIGIN OF PHRASAL VERBS

If you are curious about the origin of phrasal verbs, you've come to the right place. In this blog post, we will embark on a journey through time to uncover the history behind these confusing constructions. From their ancient beginnings to their modern application, let's explore the evolution of phrasal verbs and how they continue to entertain and challenge language learners around the world.

I. Exploring the Origin of Phrasal Verbs

English is a fascinating language, and understanding its history can help us to appreciate it more. Composing our modern-day English from a range of influences, including old English, has allowed for interesting quirks like the creation of many phrasal verbs. These combinations often trace back to short phrases that have grown in complexity over time and now serve as concise ways to express an idea or command. With an ever-evolving nature, it's no wonder the English language remains popular worldwide!

The English language is full of surprises, and some of its oldest components still come into play today! Take for example two simple phrases that date all the way back to Old English — "look out" and "stand up". Though their meanings have evolved over time, it's incredible to think that these two small words have been around for nearly a millennium! It only goes to show that the past is never too far away.

Similarly, the English language has continually evolved over time, and this is especially true when it comes to the use of phrasal verbs. In recent years these have become very commonplace in everyday speech, with new ones being invented all the time. As such, English remains a growing and versatile language with so many possibilities for expression.

II. Navigating Through English Language History

From the very first known written record of the English language in the 6th century, it has been an ever-evolving and continuously changing entity. Whether you are aware of it or not, you're actually speaking a much different language than people did centuries ago!

ARTICLE

It's quite amazing to think how far the English language has come since its humble beginnings, but one thing remains true — its gripping history shows no signs of slowing down anytime soon.

It's no secret that English has been heavily influenced by Latin, French, and other languages over the centuries. Every phrase we use today, from the simplest sentence fragment to the most complicated phrasal verb has evolved significantly since English first emerged. It's amazing how much English has changed and adapted while still remaining a part of its original roots!

Thus, the Great Vowel Shift of the fifteenth century drastically altered English pronunciation as well as leading to the formation of new words and phrases, including the popular use of phrasal verbs.

As it spread through England and eventually across the world, many people started speaking a different language than they were used to. This shift in English has had a lasting effect on how people communicate even to this day.

III. Historical Development of the English Language

It's no wonder that English is known as a beautiful and complex language; it has been evolving since the 5th century!

English began when the Anglo-Saxons brought their tongue to Britain, beginning an incredible journey of grammar and language.

Through centuries of conquests and discoveries, the English language has gone through some interesting changes and still continues to change to this day!

The English language has had quite the journey! Way back in the day, it was known as Old English — a much simpler form of the sophisticated language we know and love today.

Over time, English underwent radical changes with Latin and Norman French infiltrating to create Middle English. It's definitely come a long way and survived many transitions along the way!

In conclusion, the English language has changed dramatically since William Caxton introduced the printing press to Britain in the 15th century.

This revolutionized many aspects of language, including the creation and popularization of phrasal verbs.

The standardization of English furthered by the printing press is responsible for Modern English as we know it today.

IV. Examining Proto-Indo-European Roots

Many of us take the English language for granted, but its history is far more complex than we might think. It is believed that the root of all modern European languages goes back to a single language, known as Proto-Indo-European.

Without this original language and its many subsequent branches, our conversational landscape would look very different today — proving just how important English language history really is!

It's remarkable to think that many of the words we use in everyday speech today can trace their roots back to Old English.

By examining these ancient origins, linguists have been able to uncover clues about how words evolved over time, and what their meanings were originally used for.

It's like a journey through history — it's intriguing to see how language has changed with the culture!

Thus, gaining a comprehensive understanding of the English language requires looking back at its earliest roots in Proto-Indo-European and studying how those old English words spread and evolved over the centuries.

This can provide fascinating insight into the shared histories of different cultures, showing how languages influenced and blended with each other.

V. Analyzing the Chronology of Verbal Constructs

If you've ever been perplexed by the complex phrasal verbs of the English language, like "turn off" or "fall apart",[75]

ARTICLE

you can trace their history all the way back to Early Modern English. Examining the chronology of verbal constructs in English is a great way to understand how language has evolved over time — especially when it comes to thrilling expressions like phrasal verbs!

The English language is a constantly-evolving beast, and nowhere is that more evident than in the different forms of verbs used over the years.

From Middle English to Old Norse, even the earliest roots of some words can offer historians some interesting insight into how English has changed and grown.

The use of these older verb forms give us an impressive foundation for further understanding the history of English; without them, we'd be missing out on a wealth of knowledge!

Again, when we look at the history of English language, a deeper understanding of its origins can be explored through analyzing the usage of older verb forms such as phrasal verbs.

Doing so allows us to track how English has evolved over time and has been used in different contexts.

VI. Uncovering New Phrasal Verb Meanings

Phrasal verbs are an integral part of everyday English, and their meanings have evolved over the centuries. In fact, if you were to travel back in time and compare how we used these phrases centuries ago versus how they're used today, you'd likely be astounded at the contrast!

This is a testament to the wonderfully creative environment that has shaped English language history.

Did you know that, by examining the history of the English language, we can gain new insights into some commonly used phrases?

It's fascinating to get a glimpse into how different forms of English grammar has evolved over time.

With a bit of study, we can now better understand why certain phrasal verbs are used in conversations and literature.

Who knew that deciphering the nuances of English language history could reveal so much about day-to-day way of speaking!

Next, looking at the history of English helps us to understand why we use phrasal verbs. Through examining the history of English, we can identify how language has evolved, and how word usage has changed over time — especially in regard to phrasal verbs.

Ultimately, reflecting on the evolution of language can help us better interpret current usage and shape our own use of language in a more conscious way.

Wrapping up

In conclusion, phrasal verbs have come a long way since they were first used in Old and Middle English. From their ancient beginnings to their modern application, we've taken a journey through time to uncover the origin of phrasal verbs and how they've become such a big part of the English language today.

ARTICLE

Although they can be challenging for language learners, mastering the use of phrasal verbs is essential to becoming an advanced English speaker.

With increased practice, fascination, and understanding of these verb formations, one can make considerable strides in acquiring proficiency.

ARTICLE

HOW TO STAY MOTIVATED TO KEEP LEARNING A NEW LANGUAGE

Learning a new language is one of the most rewarding experiences you can have. There's something about the mystique of learning a new language that makes you feel like a genius.

However, new language learners often encounter problems when they try to learn a language by themselves.

One of the biggest problems with learning a language on your own is a lack of motivation. It can be quite difficult to stay motivated to learn a new language when you're doing it by yourself.

To help you stay motivated to keep your language learning on track, I've put together a list of things you can do to help yourself stay motivated to learn a new language and culture.

One of the first things that you can do to motivate yourself is to keep your goals in mind.

ARTICLE

It's much easier to get motivated to do something when you have clear goals that you're working towards.

When you start learning a language, you should have specific goals that you want to work towards. Having a clear goal in mind is a great way to keep yourself motivated to continue learning the language you're studying.

Another thing that you can do to help keep yourself motivated is to set goals for yourself that are realistic and achievable.

Setting unrealistic goals for yourself will do more harm than good in the long run.

As a result, you probably won't achieve your goals and you may get discouraged as a result.

Try to set yourself up for success by setting reasonable goals and staying on track to reach those goals.

You should also make an effort to surround yourself with people who sharethe same interests as you.

ARTICLE

Social support is very important for keeping youmotivated as you work towards your goals.

Taking a break from your studies can also be helpful when it comes to keeping your motivation levels high.

Learning something new can be hard work, and it can be easy to get burnt out if you're constantly working without a break.

Taking a break every once in a while allows you to recharge and refresh so that you can get back to learning refreshed and ready to face your next challenge head-on.

Also, you should make sure you reward yourself when you reach each of your milestones along the way.

Achieving even the smallest milestone should be celebrated because it can help you to stay motivated to keep working towards your final goal.

It's important to celebrate all of your achievements while you're learning a new language so you don't forget how far you've come since Day 1.

ARTICLE

These simple tips can help you stay motivated and help you achieve the success that you're looking for.

Many people find language learning to be quite difficult at first, but **as long as you stick with it and stay positive**, you'll eventually find that it's **not as hard as you thought it was going to be.**

17816097R00049